Name:

School:

Class:

D0319388

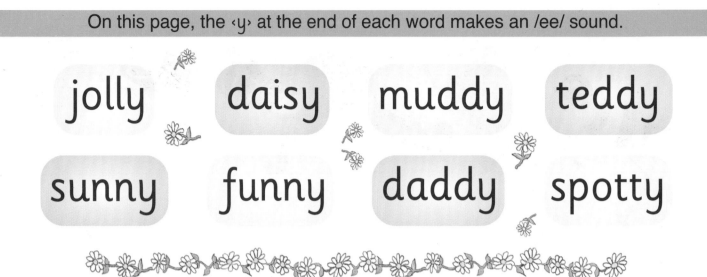

jolly   daisy   muddy   teddy

sunny   funny   daddy   spotty

Read the words in the logs. Match each word to the right picture.

sunny

body

puppy

teddy

sandy

holly

Dictation:

_____

_____

_____

_____

_____

_____

_____

_____

s a t i p n

S S S S S S

A A A A A A

T T T T T T

I I I I I I

P P P P P P

N N N N N N

Write inside the outline letters and match the capital letters to the lower case letters.

S   p   n   i   A

t   I   s

N   a   P

3

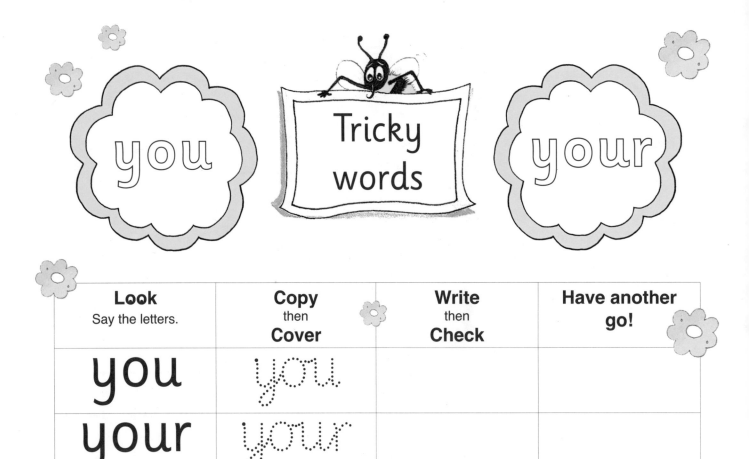

you

Tricky words

your

Look Say the letters.	Copy then **Cover**	Write then **Check**	Have another go!
you	*you*		
your	*your*		

Write inside the vowel letters using a blue pen or pencil.
Then find the vowels in the grid and colour the squares with a short vowel in blue.

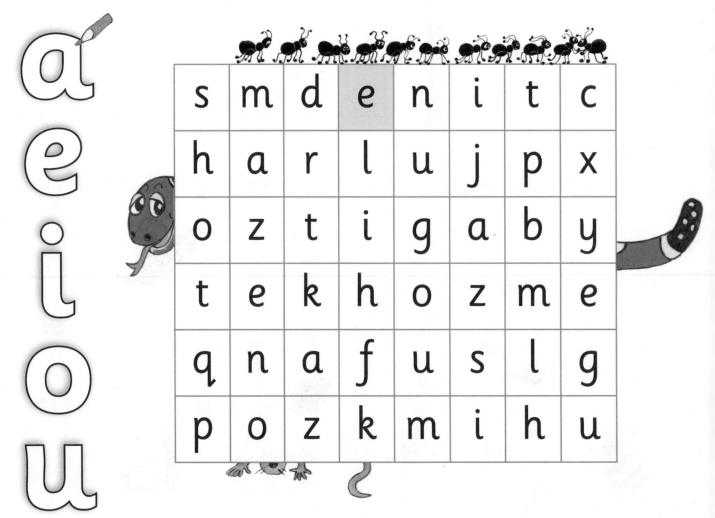

a
e
i
o
u

s	m	d	e	n	i	t	c
h	a	r	l	u	j	p	x
o	z	t	i	g	a	b	y
t	e	k	h	o	z	m	e
q	n	a	f	u	s	l	g
p	o	z	k	m	i	h	u

the hen

Choose one of the short vowel sounds, /a/, /e/, /i/, /o/, or /u/, to make the words.

f u n	h _ p	r _ d	b _ g
m _ n	p _ t	c _ p	m _ p
s _ ck	sh _ p	cl _ p	qu _ ck

a e i o u

bag net bin box mug

Ring the short vowel and write the word. Colour the pictures.

a e i **o** u

b o x

a e i o u

a e i o u

a e i o u

a e i o u

a e i o u

a e i o u

a e i o u

a e i o u

6

Dictation:

_____

_____

_____

_____

_____

_____

_____

_____

c k e h r m d

C C C C C C C

K K K K K K K

E E E E E E E

H H H H H H H

R R R R R R R

M M M M M M M

D D D D D D D

Write inside the outline letters and match the capital letters to the lower case letters.

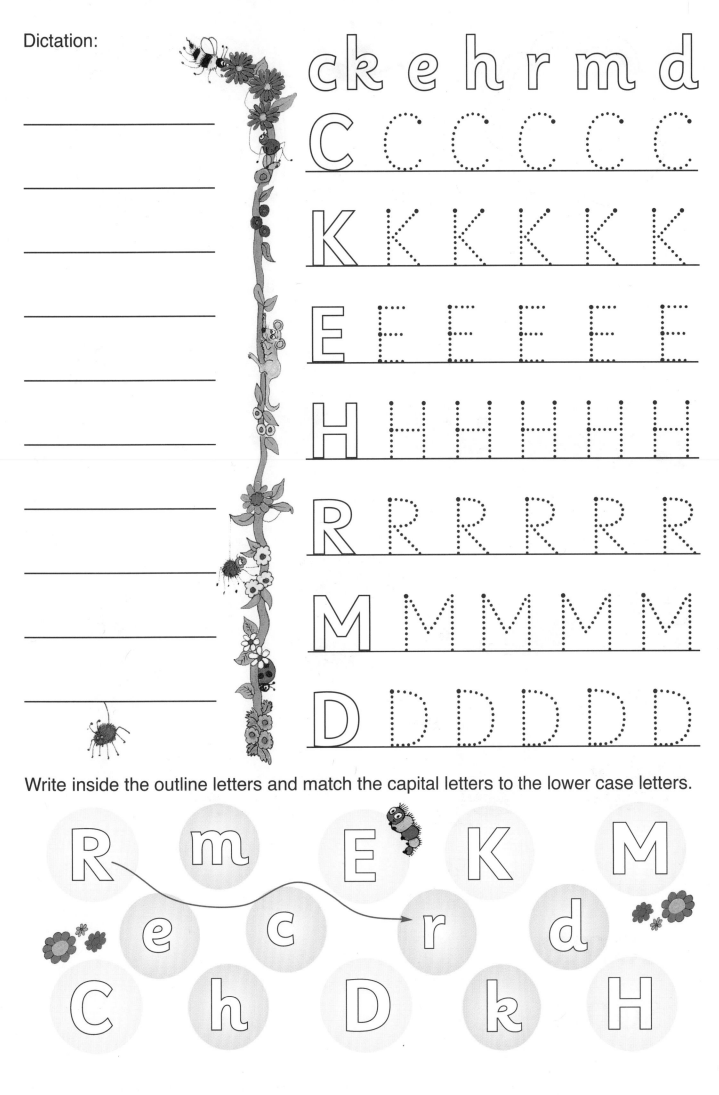

R m   E   K   M

e   c   r   d

C   h   D   k   H

come Tricky words **some**

Read the words in the flowers below and join the pairs.
Find the flowers containing the words *some* and *come* and colour these flowers yellow.

Look Say the letters.	**Copy** then **Cover**	**Write** then **Check**	**Have another go!**
come	come		
some	some		

8

in the park

Join each word to the right picture.

swing   dog   picnic   tree

duck bricks sack peck black

sock jacket tick kick clock

Write over the dotted words and draw a picture for each word in the rockets.

10

Dictation:

_____

_____

_____

_____

_____

_____

_____

_____

_____

_____

_____

_____

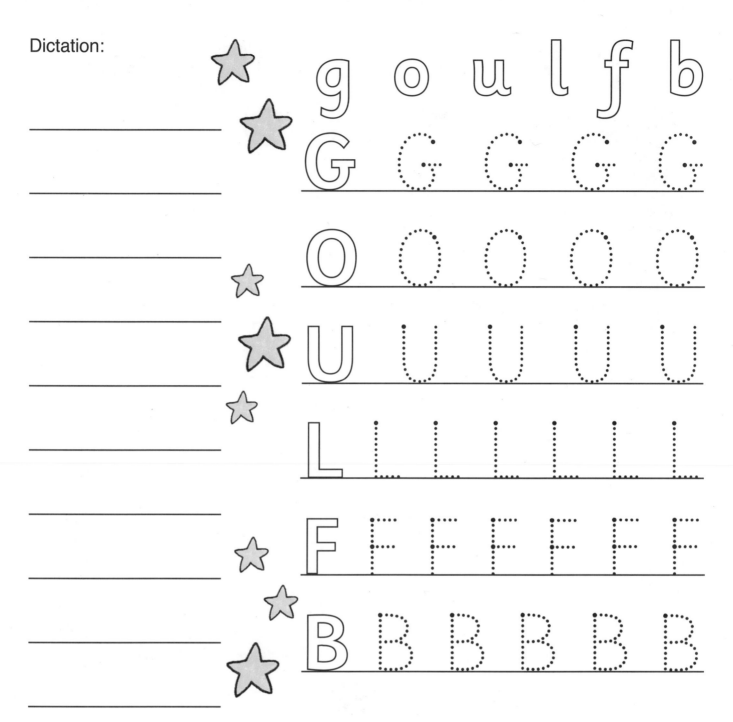

g o u l f b

G G G G G

O O O O O

U U U U U

L L L L L L L

F F F F F F F

B B B B B B

Match the capital letters to the lower case letters.

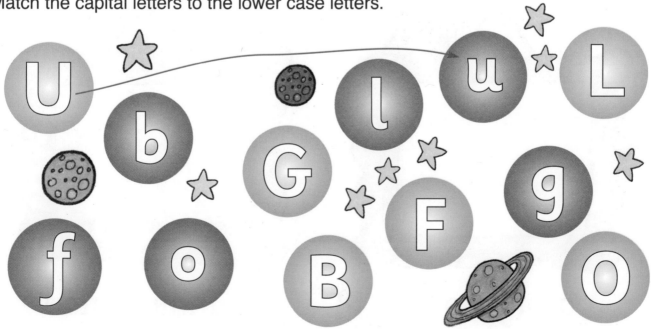

Read each phrase and draw a picture in the frame to illustrate it.

a spotty dog

a fluffy cat

a green frog

an oak tree

a big clock

a running man

said

here

there

Look Say the letters.	**Copy** then **Cover**	**Write** then **Check**	**Have another go!**
said	said		
here	here		
there	there		

Write the word underneath each picture. Colour the pictures.

b e d

the pond

Join each word to the right picture.

rocks   duckling   toad   boat

When two letters that make the same sound are next to each other, the sound is only said once.

parrot   egg   bell   jazz   button

kitten   huff   bill   doll   miss

Read the word and draw a picture to go with it.

rabbit

dress

duck

shell

puppet

carrot

Dictation:

_____

_____

_____

_____

_____

_____

_____

_____

Write inside the capital letters and join them to the matching lower-case letters.

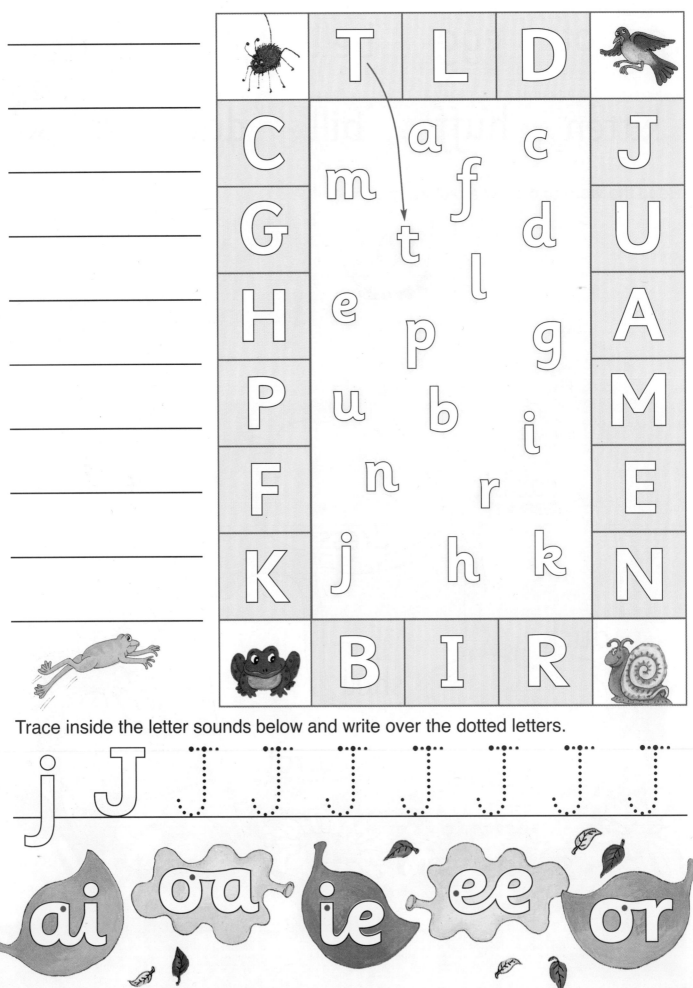

Trace inside the letter sounds below and write over the dotted letters.

j J J ·J· ·J· ·J· ·J· ·J· ·J· ·J·

ai   oa   ie   ee   or

Tricky words

they

Look Say the letters.	Copy then Cover	Write then Check	Have another go!
they	they		

Choose the right word and write it underneath the picture.

met mat man
mat

log dig dog
_ _ _

cup cut cap
_ _ _

peg egg pig
_ _ _

net nut not
_ _ _

and ant act
_ _ _

three trick tree
_ _ _

boot book boat
_ _ _

jar jet jam
_ _ _

the fox

Join each word to the right picture.

red   fox   nest   bat

In words with a 'hop-over e' digraph, the ‹e› at the end does not say /e/; it uses its magic to hop back over the consonant and turns the short vowel into a long vowel sound.

smoke   use   game   eve   mule

hive   these   joke   shave   side

Join each leaf to the right tree.

Dictation: _____

Write inside each outline letter and then write its matching upper or lower case letter in the space next to it.

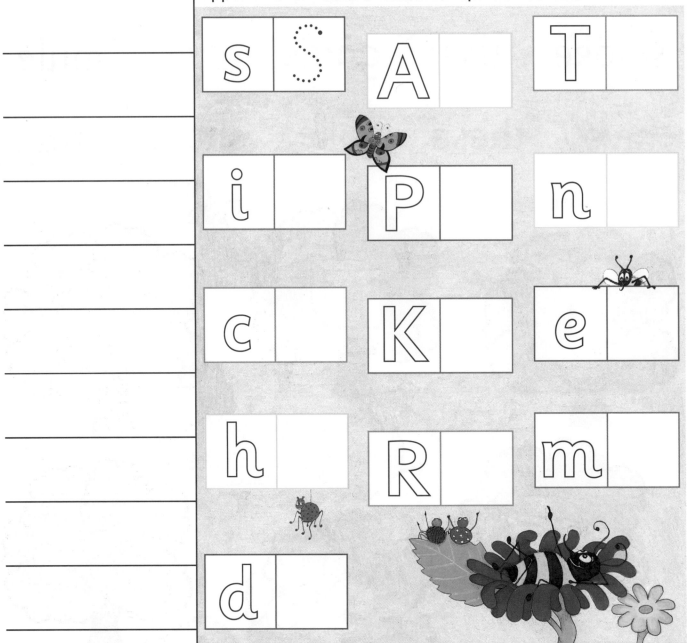

Write inside the outline letters and then write over the dotted capital letters.

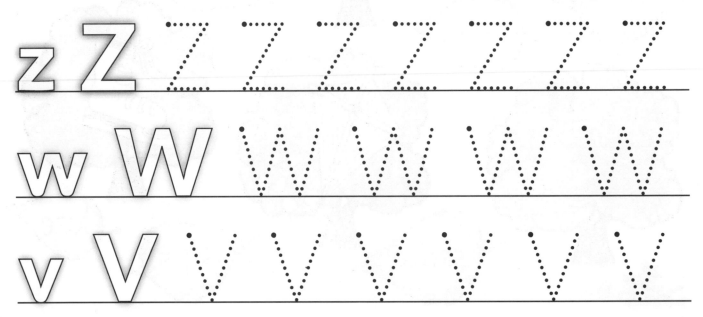

go

Tricky words

no   so

Read the words and then find them in the wordsearch.

your   here   go

no   they

said   so

there   some

you   come

a	c	o	m	e	b	s	o
s	a	i	d	d	t	p	f
n	o	p	a	y	o	u	m
h	e	r	e	c	d	x	z
q	u	m	t	h	e	r	e
y	o	u	r	f	h	g	o
k	s	j	x	t	h	e	y
c	z	s	o	m	e	r	w

Look Say the letters.	Copy then **Cover**	Write then **Check**	Have another go!
go	go		
no	no		
so	so		

the fish

Match each word to the right sea creature.

catfish   starfish   flatfish   eel

22

Dictation: _____

Write the upper or lower case letter in the space next to its matching letter.

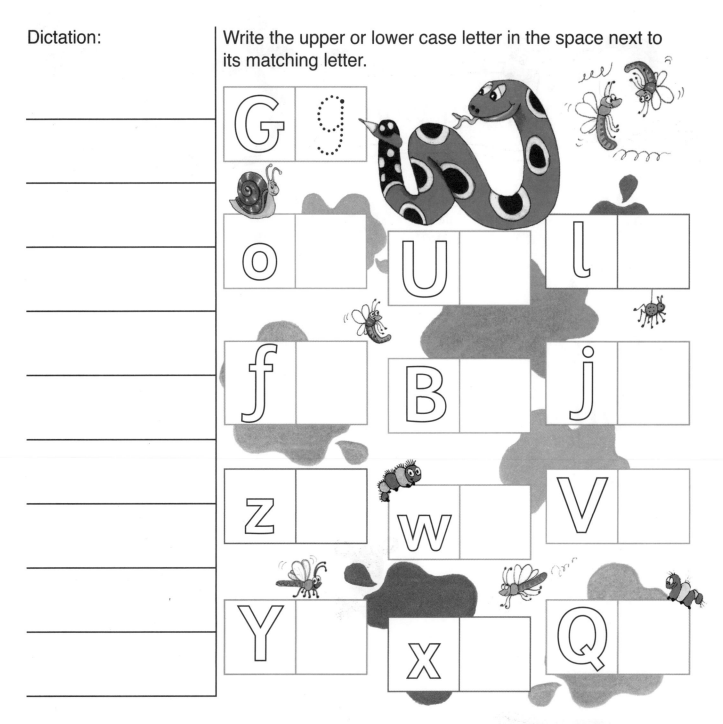

Write inside the outline letters and then write over the dotted capital letters.

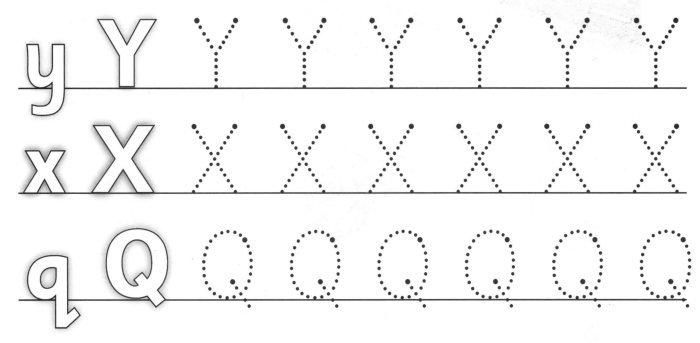

my

Tricky words

one   by

Look Say the letters.	Copy then Cover	Write then Check	Have another go!
my	my		
one	one		
by	by		

Look at each picture and then write the word underneath.

cue

_____

_____

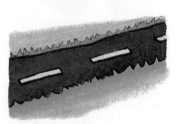

_____

_____

_____

_____

_____

_____

24

night
time

Join each word to the right picture.

star   moth   sleeping   moon

Choose the right spelling of the /ai/ sound for each picture.

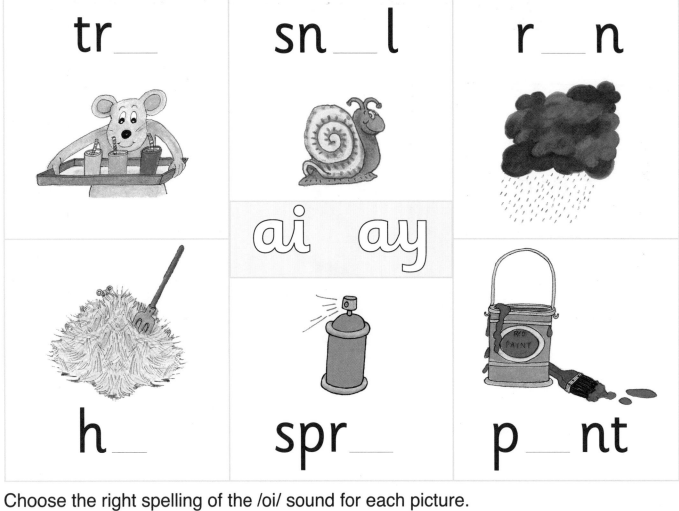

tr___

sn___l

r___n

ai ay

h___

spr___

p___nt

Choose the right spelling of the /oi/ sound for each picture.

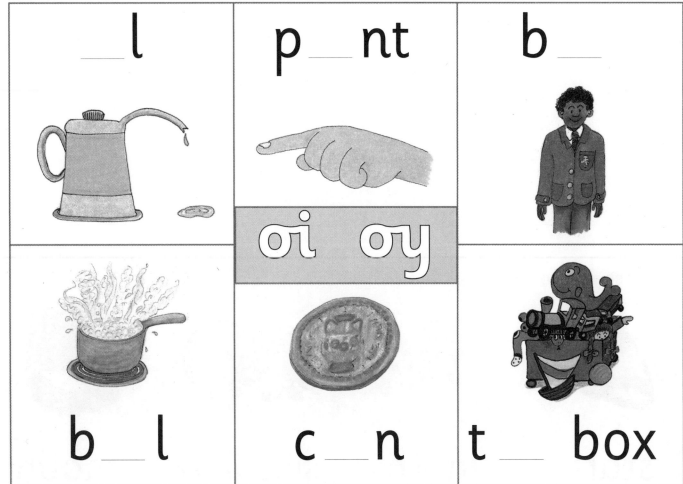

___l

p___nt

b___

oi oy

b___l

c___n

t___box

26

Dictation:

_____

_____

_____

_____

_____

_____

_____

Write the sections of the alphabet in red, yellow, green or blue.

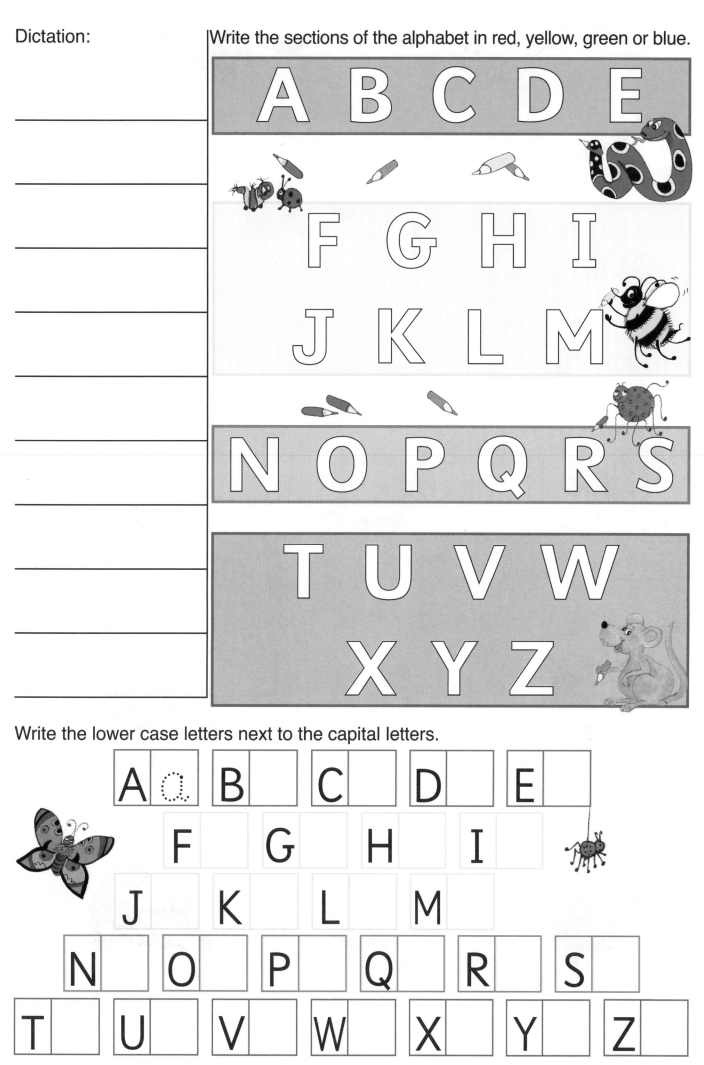

A B C D E

F G H I

J K L M

N O P Q R S

T U V W

X Y Z

Write the lower case letters next to the capital letters.

A a   B   C   D   E

F   G   H   I

J   K   L   M

N   O   P   Q   R   S

T   U   V   W   X   Y   Z

27

Look	Copy	Write	Have another
Say the letters.	then Cover	then Check	go!
only	*only*		
old	*old*		

Animal anagrams: put the letters in the right order.

ant	n t a	snail	n s ai l	goat	g t oa
sheep	ee p sh	shark	k ar sh	crab	r b a c
yak	k a y	chick	i ch c k	fox	o f x

ducks

Animal anagrams: put the letters in the right order.

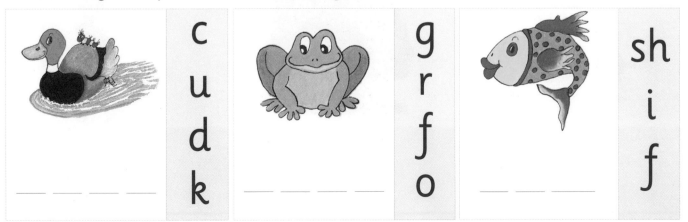

c u d k

g r f o

sh i f

Read the words at the top of the page and write the correct word under each picture.

three   teeth   tree

leaf   feet   sheep

seal   bee   sea

sheep

___ ___ ___ ___

___ ___ ___ ___

___ ___ ___ ___

___ ___ ___ ___

___ ___ ___ ___

___ ___ ___ ___

___ ___ ___ ___

Dictation:

_____

_____

_____

_____

_____

_____

_____

_____

Write the upper case letter next to the lower case letter.

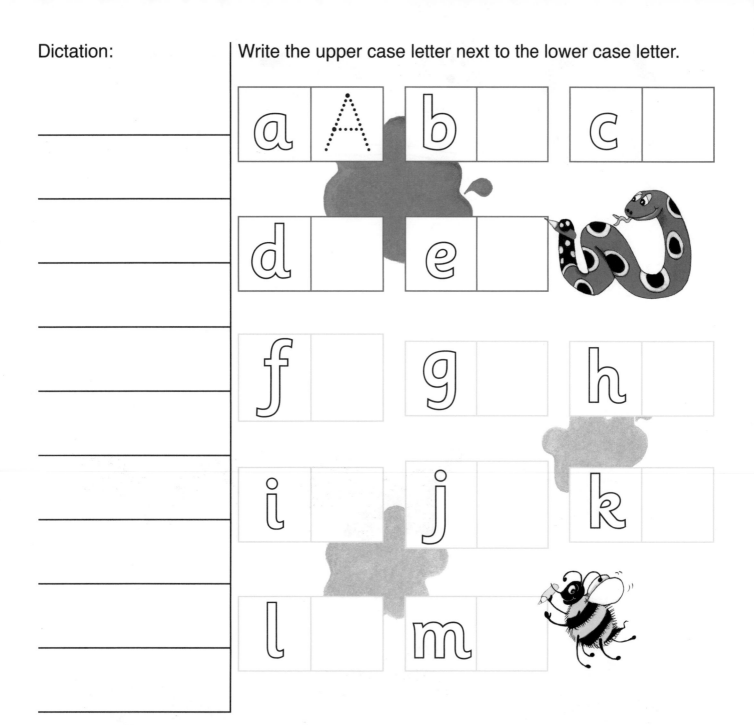

| a | A | b | | c | |

| d | | e | |

| f | | g | | h | |

| i | | j | | k | |

| l | | m | |

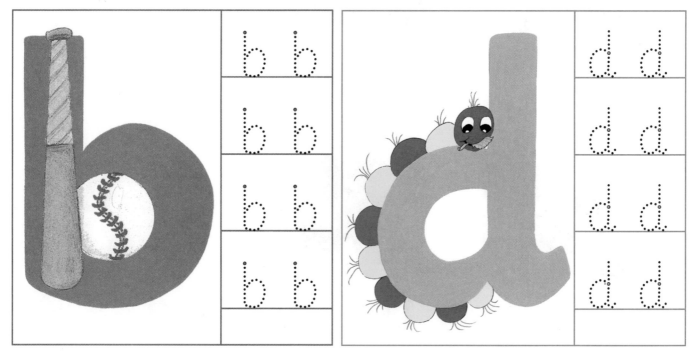

b	b
b	b
b	b
b	b

d	d
d	d
d	d
d	d

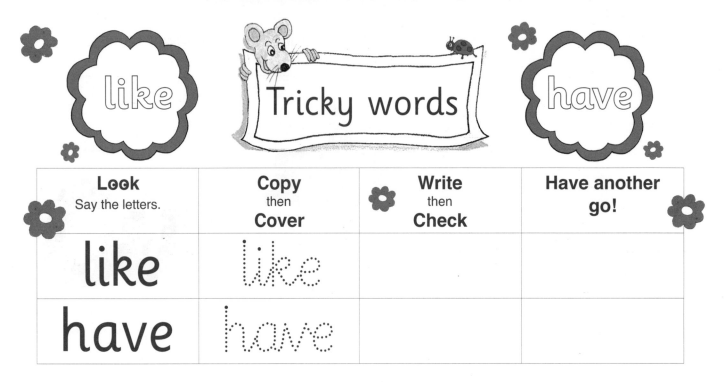

Tricky words

Look Say the letters.	**Copy** then **Cover**	**Write** then **Check**	**Have another go!**
like	like		
have	have		

Look at the pictures and choose a /b/ or /d/ sound.

b e d

_og

_at

cra_

pon_

_ook

win_y

te_ _y

ra_ _it

the queen

Practise writing ‹b› and ‹d›.

b b b b b b b b

d d d d d d d

pie   lie   line   time   my   flying

tried   cries   sunshine   shy   sky

tie   die   drive   slide   drying   try

Read the words in the stars and draw pictures in the moons to illustrate each word.

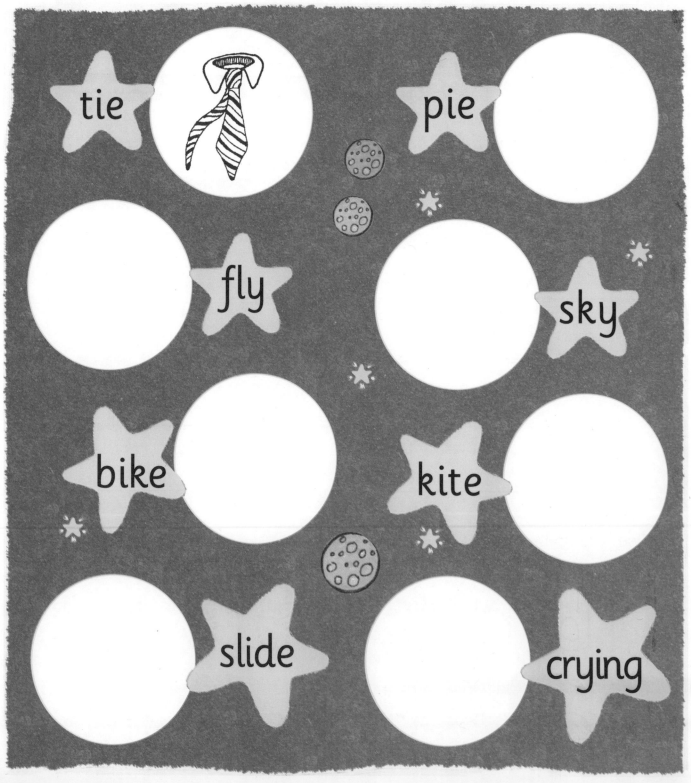

tie   pie

fly   sky

bike   kite

slide   crying

Dictation:

_____

_____

_____

_____

_____

_____

_____

_____

Write the upper-case letter next to the lower-case letter.

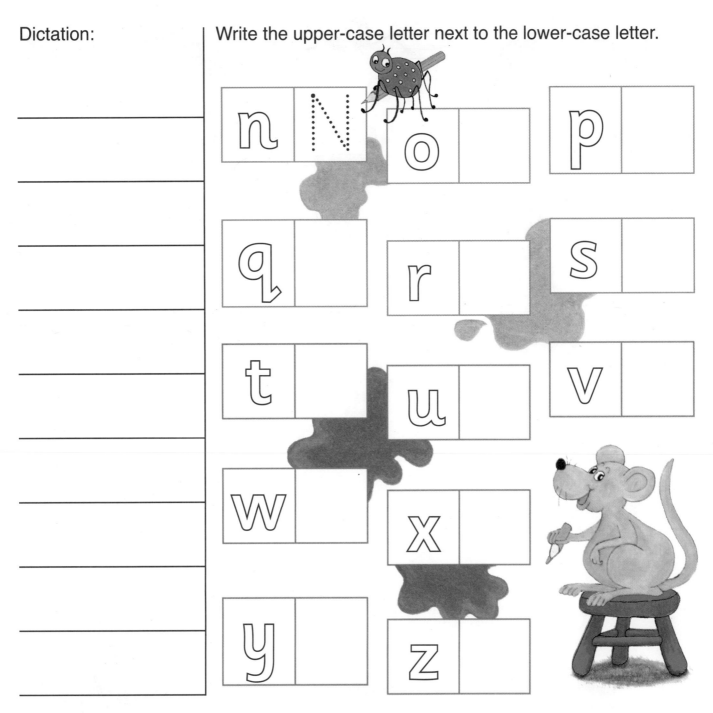

Read each sentence and draw a picture in the frame to illustrate it.

The sun is hot.

She is running.

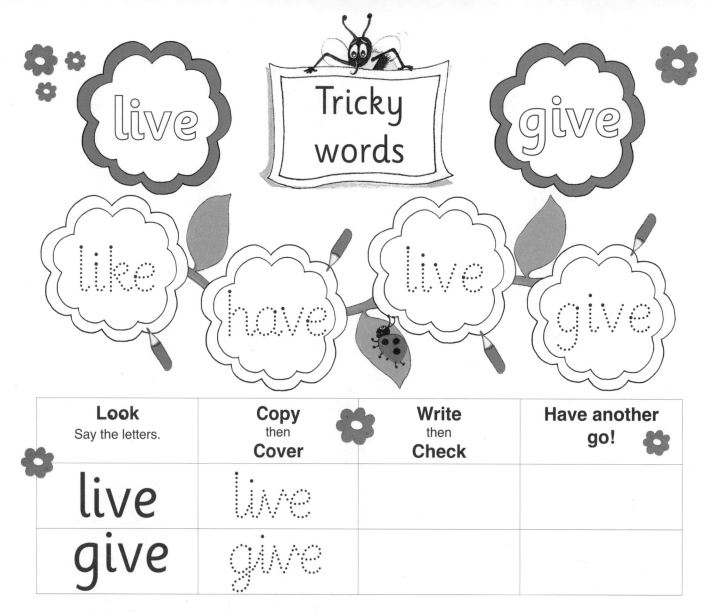

Tricky words

live

give

like

have

live

give

Look Say the letters.	**Copy** then **Cover**	**Write** then **Check**	**Have another go!**
live	live		
give	give		

Choose the right word and write it underneath the picture.

cub   cube

fin   fine

hug   huge

_____

tub   tube

hat   hate

rid   ride

_____

digging
for
treasure

Write over these 'caterpillar c' shapes.

shout south
mouse flour

town brown
owl flower

Read each word inside the clouds and boats and draw a picture to illustrate it.

cloud

owl

crown

boat

snow

arrow

coat toad
oak soap

grow borrow
yellow slow

Dictation:

_____

_____

_____

_____

_____

_____

_____

_____

Revise writing these 'caterpillar c' letters.

c c c c · · ·

a a a a · ·

d d d d · ·

o o o o · ·

g g g g · ·

q q q q · ·

Look at each picture and write the word underneath. Colour the pictures.

_____   _____   _____

little

Tricky words

down

Read the words and then find them in the wordsearch.

one

my

by

only

old

down

little

like

give

live

have

l	i	k	e	n	b	m	y
d	f	g	h	a	v	e	f
d	o	w	n	l	i	v	e
o	n	e	s	c	b	y	z
g	u	m	t	s	e	r	u
o	l	d	r	o	n	l	y
k	s	g	i	v	e	r	p
j	p	l	i	t	t	l	e

Look Say the letters.	Copy then Cover	Write then Check	Have another go!
little	little		
down	down		

40

the shipwreck

_____

_____

_____

_____

_____

_____

Match each word to the right sea creature.

  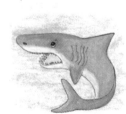 

crab　　　shells　　　lobster　　　shark

Sound out each word and draw a picture inside the shape.

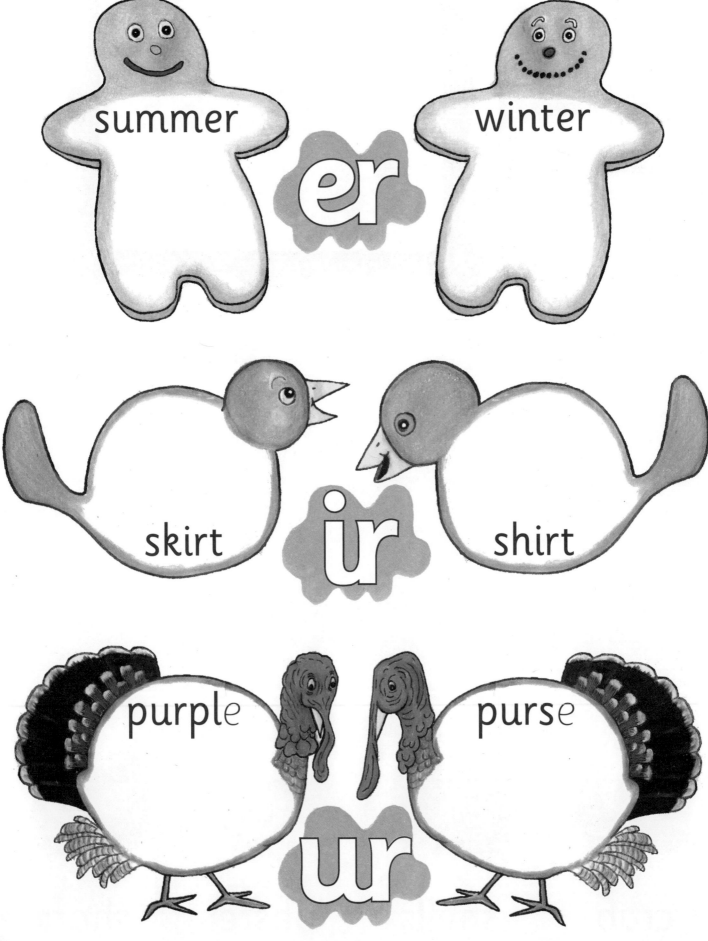

summer

winter

er

skirt

shirt

ir

purple

purse

ur

Dictation:

Revise writing the tall letters.

_____

_____

_____

_____

_____

_____

_____

_____

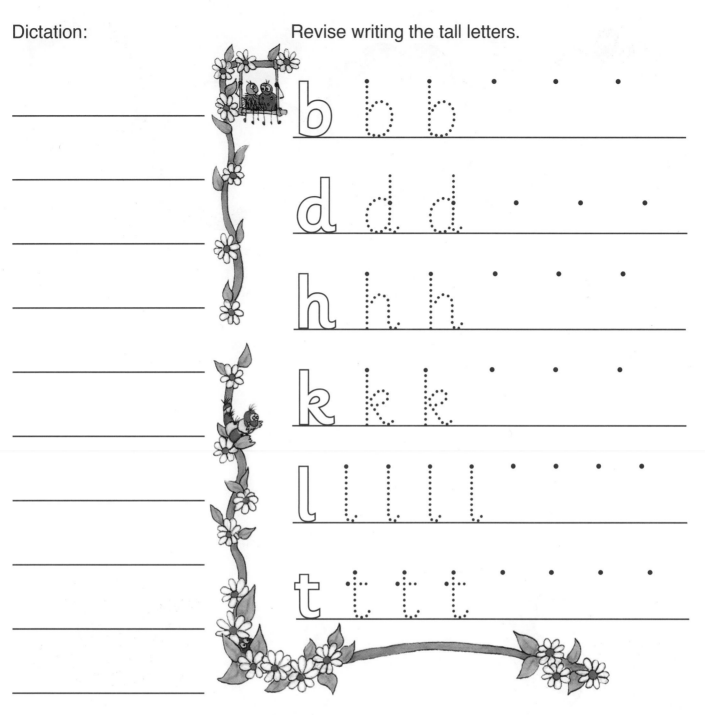

b b b · · ·

d d d · · ·

h h h · · ·

k k k · · ·

l l l l l · · · ·

t t t t · · · ·

Fill in the spaces and shade in the letters.

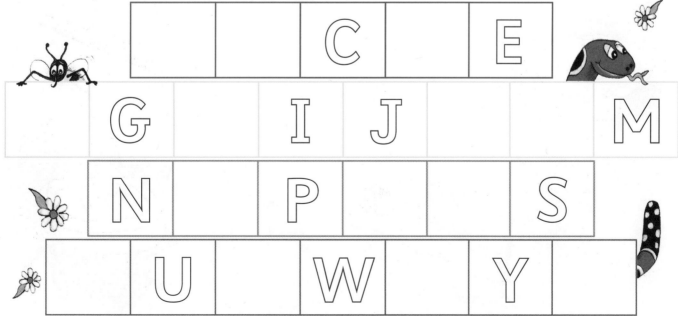

| | | C | | E |
| | | | | |

| G | | I | J | | M |

| N | | P | | S |

| U | | W | | Y |

what

when

why

Look Say the letters.	**Copy** then **Cover**	**Write** then **Check**	**Have another go!**
what	what		
when	when		
why	why		

Join each word to the right picture and then colour in the pictures.

lie

tree

nail

leek

snail

soap

road

pie

helping
to fix
the car

Join each word to the right vehicle.

bus   jeep   van   car

Dictation:

_____

_____

_____

_____

_____

_____

_____

_____

_____

Revise writing these long letters.

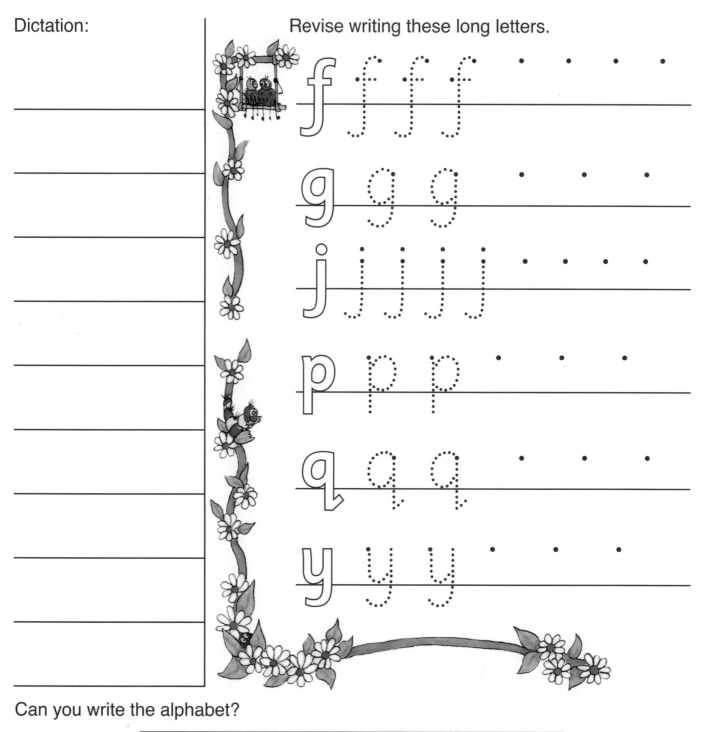

f f f f · · · ·

g g g · · ·

j j j j · · ·

p p p · · ·

q q q · · ·

y y y · · ·

Can you write the alphabet?

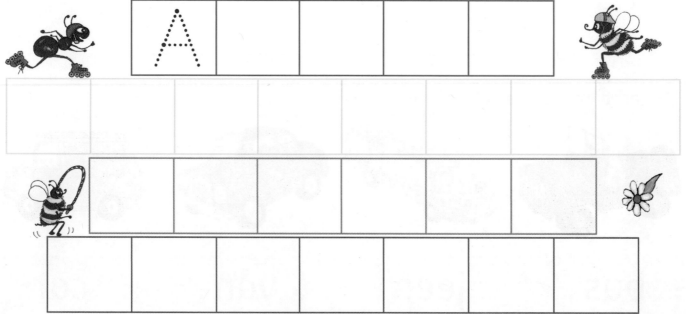

A

where

Tricky words

who   which

Look Say the letters.	Copy then Cover	Write then Check	Have another go!
where	where		
who	who		
which	which		

Read each sentence and draw a picture in the frame to illustrate it.

I see the moon and stars.

A boy is asleep in bed.

A duck is swimming
on the pond.

The girl has a green
dress.

the statue

_____

_____

_____

_____

_____

Join each word to the right picture.

tie   lamb   bird   boot